A slightly different version of "The Wasted Year—1984" was published by *Okike*, 27/28, March 1988, under the name Lynn Nwuneli.

"to be come a man" and "untitled, unwritten" appeared in 1985 issues of the *Nigerwives Newsletter*, as did "under-cover", then entitled "morning glory".

University of Lagos Press
1999

This book is dedicated in memory of
Gloria Jinadu,
who gave so many people so much,
and to all the Ashoka Fellows;
may they continue to embody the same spirit.

Archetyping

Poems

Lynn Chukura

Published by the University of Lagos Press,
University of Lagos,
Akoka, Lagos, Nigeria.

ISBN 978-017-055-3

Printed in Nigeria by the University of Lagos Press
01-825048

Acknowledgements

The author is grateful to all the friends and colleagues who have read her poems, made useful suggestions, and encouraged her to carry on.

Although those who have been helpful in the past or present are too many to name individually, special thanks are due to Prof. 'Biodun Adetugbo, Karen King-Aribisala, Harry Garuba, Odia Ofeimun, Nina Mba, Edwina Salako, the late Prof. Fred Nnabuenyi Ugonna and his wife, Judy Ugonna, Sr. Majella McCarron, and irreplaceable Ken, who was the first to laugh.

Most of all to be thanked is Tony Dadzie, perceptive reader and critic of everything I've done, for offering to write the Introduction.

Contents

INTRODUCTION IX

THE WOMAN'S PAGE 17

LOVE 18
THE OLD WIVES' TALE 19
DONNA JUANITA 20
UNTITLED, UNWRITTEN 21
OFF BEAT 22
EARTHMOTHER 23
FEMININITY 24
CLOSE 25
TO IAGO INTERNALISED 26
SISTERHOOD 28
DISMISSED 29
ANIMUS 30

TYPE CAST 31

BABY IN GLASSES 32
LABELS 33
THE NIGERIAN MALE 34
DEHUMANISED 35

QUIXOTE 36
LESSONS 38
TIME WARP I 39
TIME WARP II 40
UNDER-COVER 41
TO BE COME A MAN 42
THE ASTUTE PICKLE 44
PRIMA DONNA 45
GLAMOUR GIRL 46

INSIDE THE IVORY TOWER 47

DECONSTRUCTION 48
D*E*E*P G*R*A*M*M*A*R 49
ON TEACHING AFRO-AMERICAN POETRY TO AFRICAN STUDENTS 51
RETURN OF THE LECTURER 52
HOME IS WHERE THE DOORS CLOSE 55
THE WASTED YEAR 59
I. *THE BURIAL OF THE FAILED* 60
II. *A GAME OF CHARADES* 63
III. *WHAT THE EXAMS SAID* 65
NOTES ON *THE WASTED YEAR* 69

Introduction

Although not a literary specialist, I offered to write this introduction after reading the poems in this volume, because of how much I enjoyed them. I therefore invite you to join me in a voyage of discovery to savour the pleasures of these poems.

I was delighted by the deft touches with which the poet, Lynn Chukura, conveys meaning, and the often playful way in which she treats her themes. Her focus is humanity, particularly women, whose roles have been defined and fixed from as long as we can think. She asks us to re-examine our preconceptions from uncustomary perspectives. I was also delighted by the tone of mock seriousness with which she parodies long-held beliefs about human behaviour, and by the variety of styles which she employs.

Chukura uses language with the wit and skill of a virtuoso, and rereading her poems reveals layers of meaning which may elude the casual reader. A book which not only gives immediate pleasure, but also bears rereading, and provides fresh insights each time, is a good book. *Archetyping* does all of this.

A closer look at the structure and contents of the volume follows. But if you find it heavy going, why not turn straight to the poems?

****

Archetyping is a volume of poems in which the author combines three related concepts—the archetype, the stereotype and type casting, all of which are products of human "understanding" of the nature of others in interactive situations. The word 'archetyping' is a blend of all three concepts, which invites us to critically examine our assumptions about human roles and types, see their shortcomings and recognise the deleterious effect that an unquestioning acceptance of their validity may have on the psyche, particularly, the female psyche.

Archetyping

Archetypes are universal human types from which are derived models of behaviour and ways of conceiving alternative patterns of human interaction. They may even be considered as human prototypes, and provide a means of identifying the central impetus behind various kinds of behaviour.

The psychologist Carl Jung, who popularised the term, explores archetypes as psychic forces that operate in the unconscious and are expressed in dreams, literature and mythology. In a given society some of them are favoured as models of behaviour and invoked to assess the behaviour of others. Some are held up as examples of unacceptable behaviour yet represent something within us, and therefore still elicit a powerful response. Eshu in the Yoruba pantheon is a Trickster and is admired for his ingenuity and pranks. We also have the Hero who does marvellous things and is a model of achievement. Other archetypes include Prince Charming, the Femme Fatale, Earth Mother, the Healer, the Stranger—variations of which may be identified in all societies and which appear also in folklore and literature.

It is from narratives that, consciously or unconsciously, we take patterns for our lives and form our ideas of how we expect others to behave. The author asks us to re-examine some of these moulds of human life and consider which of them may be a source of strength, and which may, and in what circumstances, be deleterious, especially when imposed rather than chosen.

Stereotypes are preconceived generalisations held by members of one group about another. They downplay diversity and individuality, for the sake of providing a simplified way of responding to others. However, imposing one's stereotypes on others has dehumanising and offensive effects.

'Type casting' refers originally to theatre and films, when an actor finds his choices of parts to play severely limited by assumptions about his strengths and limitations. Chukura uses the concept metaphorically to represent the effect of stereotyping as felt by the individual victim.

Chukura's word 'archetyping' combines all these concepts and invites us to see where one shades into the other and to what extent they help us better to understand social roles and interactions. This title in itself can be read as a poem—evocative and daringly combining multiple meanings in a single coinage.

Similarly, attention should be given to the titles of the sections and individual poems in the collection for their full effect to be felt. For example, '*The Woman's Page*' could be easily passed over. But a little reflection shows that it is a deliberate choice—a condensed poem in itself which criticises the attitude that women, like children, need a newspaper page where subjects of importance only to them can be treated, leaving more serious topics for the rest of the newspaper. You can skip this page as it treats only mundane matters that hardly touch on the *real* issues. The Woman's Page in newspapers reflects a stereotyped image of women's lives, hardly touching the strains, the sense of isolation, indeed the debilitating effect of stereotyping the woman. Of course, the implied male is also stereotyped—he sees nothing significant in a woman, except perhaps in relationship to himself!

Chukura sees the problem and provides us with an intellectual lens through which to observe women and examine the traditional roles assigned to them. She does this most of the time by heightening a situation in order to dramatise its problematic aspect, as in such poems as "earth mother", "Donna Juanita", and "the old wives' tale"

"Donna Juanita" shows the housewife (a stereotype) reflecting on her 40 years of monotonous drudgery, aware that no one recognises her efforts to please others and fit herself to an unsatisfying role:

> the rhythmic demand
> of appetite, housekeeping, marital embrace
> in their narrow range of variations.

Is this unrelieved tedium all a woman is fit for? Even when her worth seems to be appreciated, she is rewarded with sops, which she has been mentally conditioned to accept. Meanwhile, where is her male counterpart—the better known Don Juan!—and is *his* life more rewarding?

Chukura is concerned with sometimes subtle abuses of women and their relegation to passive and secondary roles. "Earth mother", for example, is her rendition of a familiar score. The woman is seen only as a source of life and nurture, taken for granted by those who rely on her, until she explodes in anger and frustration. The finality of the explosion is orchestrated as we are taken through a minefield of carefully chosen words which drive us towards the inescapable. She draws our attention to '*erupt*' as in a volcano seething underground and exploding when the pressure becomes uncontainable; the once submissive woman changes. What is left to the imagination is the surprise that overwhelms the spouse who has been brought up and has lived to expect a placid woman who invariably does his bidding and whose duty is to give of herself to please.

The shape of the poem itself is emblematic of a volcanic mountain. It is carefully organised, showing even the fissures through which the molten mass moves on its way upwards before the final explosion which is usually preceded by warning rumbles. Chukura provides another example of concrete poetic structure in "off beat poet of the body", where the poem visually reproduces the female form to reinforce her theme of the vagaries of the body (see also "femininity").

Her experiences are the source of many of her poems. Such experiences are deeply felt as they affect one of the fundamental concerns of this volume—the effect of being 'typecast' on the feminine psyche. *Type Cast* contains four poems that show how these experiences affect a woman's life, amusing, frustrating, exasperating, and driving her sometimes to rage. "Labels" tells us about the constrictive effect that labelling can have on the individual (the female is never far away in these poems). Other labels—"men only", "our wife", "oyinbo", "CIA"—confront the individual who is only recognised by the label applied—a superficial identification tag that ignores the person's essence and relies on a second-hand knowledge of what others assume one is or should be.

In this poem, as well as in the majority of Chukura's poems, her personal experiences are the reference points from where she examines social situations. Both *The Woman's Page* and *Type Cast* sections do this consistently. Only the superficial reader will see her poems simply as a description of her personal experiences. See, for example, all the poems in *The Woman's Page*, particularly, "dismissed", and "untitled, unwritten". Other poems in *Typecast* also reflect this, as in "time warp" I & II.

The final section, *Inside the Ivory Tower*, contains poems coming from Chukura's experiences as a university teacher. Here she turns her wit on the obsession of university disciplines with new theories and the creation of new terminologies which soon become fads. Indeed, these paradigms are sometimes treated as articles of faith. There are clear references to religion in the choice of vocabulary e.g. 'dogma' 'missionary zeal', 'preach his omnipotent agent and object'. Although light-hearted, "Deep Grammar" criticises the pressures toward conformity and obscurity within the various academic disciplines.

Looking at the title, "Deep Grammar", one thinks at once of Chomsky, and transformational grammar. 'Deep Grammar' is not a transformational grammar term, but 'deep structure' is. However, 'Deep Grammar' appears to have been carefully chosen to reflect the pretensions of linguists to profound thought when considering their pet topics, with a play on the Nigerian expression 'big grammar' The poem suggests that linguists bandy esoteric terms around and expect the uninitiated to be awed and intimidated. Chukura must have gone through some pain learning the intricacies of Transformational Generative Grammar to saturate the poem with punningly accurate applications of the terminology as she does here.

I also find "return of the lecturer" interesting. Here we are exposed to the poet's imaginative way of portraying the self-critical aspect of American literature, while she hopes to awake the critical consciousness of her students. She convenes a happening and characterises each of the writers' sensibilities, however parodied this may be. Indeed, parody has a way of revealing what is missing in a situation or individual even as it exaggerates. Students find all of this too much and misunderstand, but literature, like its subject, lives on!

This section also lambastes the neglected state of university accommodation and the mentality of the academic who accepts the very worst conditions and continues to plod on. Once again, Chukura is angry with the servile stereotype that the academic has accepted, hence the medieval references in "Home is where the doors close"

"The Wasted Year", the long poem which concludes this volume, is a line-by-line parody of T.S. Eliot's *The Waste Land*, an époque–defining poem. The poem contains all the elements of the original, down to the notes, and should be read along with it to thoroughly appreciate its achievement and see the quality of the mind of the poet in her ability to parody, in a Nigerian context, this watershed in English poetry. A lecturer is driven finally to embrace madness in order to find any sense in what her students write. Many a lecturer will empathise here!

Like the section title, the lead poem of each section gives a foretaste of what is to follow, and "deconstruction", the lead poem in the last section, aptly summarises in three lines the central theme of the volume. What emerges is the author's tenet, which is to be wary of generalisations, rigid theories and ideologies which blind people to the reality of situations, be they personal, academic or interpersonal. She affirms that reality is invariably more complex than we suppose.

All the poems in this volume but one are in free verse, but free verse that allows the author to exploit rhythm to reflect the mood and general ambience of the poems. In the more prosaic poems e.g. 'off beat poet of the body', there is a conversational, almost colloquial, rhythm, which contributes to the sense of immediacy as the poet tellingly reveals the private sensations a woman goes through, and her conflicting feelings about being a woman. The same effect of immediacy is achieved in the "time warp" poems.

Other poems use rhythm to achieve different effects. In "earth mother", for example, we see a manipulation of rhythms to express moods. The poem begins with a leisurely rhythm in the vocative, addressing the archetypal "earth mother", extolling her nurturing, self-abnegating virtues. It moves steadily into a staccato rhythm as resentment builds up, ending in the volcanic eruption—and one even hears her scream.

Chukura's choice of metaphor and imagery is informed by her keen sense of observation, as well as her wide range of cultural references. In addition to the literary, we find reference to everyday things e.g. her powerful images in *Quixote* in which she talks about "lance-lean form" which not only tells us about the character's physical appearance but also refers to his militancy in defence of the ideal. There is also the "rending of power and glory into confetti" which evokes a shredding machine.

Meaning is packed tightly in seemingly innocuous phrases and metaphors. In "the old wives' tale" we find

> sanitised telling hushes aftermaths
>
> .....
>
> longing to throw open gate jammed
> by resistance of overgrowth.

Such evocative expressions as "hushes aftermaths" "throw open gate jammed", "resistance of overgrowth" render events *after* the advent of Prince Charming and the requisite happy ending of fairy tales such as "Sleeping Beauty", and simultaneously suggest an awakened but frustrated female sexuality which is left out of such conventional tales.

"Animus" is also an example of the choice of *le mot juste*, combining its general and specialised (Jungian) meanings. In Chukura's poems a deeply felt emotion finds expression in tightly controlled lines. Choices of dense metaphors like

the quicksand of negatives reasserted

challenge our imagination and our ability to conceptualise. This collection provides us with a rich reservoir of pleasure if we take time to savour such phrases.

Most of the time, particularly in the overtly feminist poems, a male reader gets the impression that only one side of the case is presented. The man is typecast and we come to expect nothing but negative behaviour from him. It is easy to write the poet off as anti-male, but this is exactly what she is against—generalisations. Perhaps she intends to right an imbalance rather than to be wholly objective. The choice of this type of male is deliberate, I would like to believe, so that other kinds of men may be thrown into relief and be a foil to their traditional counterpart.

A.B.K. Dadzie
Dept. of English, University of Lagos
June, 1998

The Woman's Page

love

the gardener tends her seedling, not
despising unopened foliage, spindly stalk,
cherishes what the plant
does not dream it can be,
raises it toward the maturity
of her own vision.

the old wives' tale

in sanctioned version comes prince
charming the euphemism for potent
hacks through bramble-forests of safeguards
camouflaging sleeping princess's rich castle
from casual passers-by.
thorns penetrated, lone footstep
moves unerringly to kiss.
castle erupts alive, commencing
feast of happily ever after.

sanitised telling hushes aftermaths
where prince moves on; where princess,
grateful or not for awakening,
keeps drawbridge lowered hospitably
to wayfarers of her own choosing.

in times to come, speak rather of
princess stirred awake by restless dreams,
longing to throw open gate jammed
by resistance of overgrowth, discovers
within the implements for her need,
swathes way to the outside herself,
laying path of her own journey's beginning.

Archetyping

Donna Juanita

entering the year of her *quarantième*
sat among the egg-smeared crockery
and considered life
in perspective of what early marriage
and toddlers sprung to teens had taught:
Nature cyclical and endlessly repetitive,
marked by rhythmic demands
of appetite, housekeeping, marital embrace
in their narrow range of variations,
borders of domestic security defended by
diligent renewal of diets and the beauty parlour—
reaching after an abstract ideal
imposed by journalistic neoplatonists
as feminine ladder of aspiration—
self-acceptance difficult to distinguish from
stagnation.
If she were to renounce effort,
the one-way slope would assert itself,
the skull beneath the made-up face.
To halt, reflect, weigh the elusiveness
of safety and all the maintenance work required
—she found it daunting.
But hidden message of the dustcloth
is defeat foreordained. Dust conquers all.
Juanita considered what a great good girl
she had been. Who would reward her
and with what recognition?
GOOD WIFE AND MOTHER AWARD
and eulogies she would have to die to hear.

untitled, unwritten

A room of one's own, said Virginia Wolf,
is requisite.
Would-be women writers
hunch grimly over the dining table
scribbling scenes
among the crumbs...
Turn that damn t.v. down!
...crouch along one edge of a bed
elbows propping head above the creative sheet...
When will you turn the light off?
sagging, sagging to sleep.

A poem may compress to such space—
never *War and Peace*.
So we learn about Anna Karenina,
Lady Chatterley and Tess
from men.
No reader wants four hundred pages
of a housewife's life
—particularly other housewives—
unless an Erma Bombeck
squeezes humour from the pits.

Archetyping

off beat
poet of the
body

as
feminists
we are all aware
of our duty to love
our bodies, particularly
their cycles of productivity &
self-cleansing, long loathed by
unenlightened men; to feel proud
of our inborn female rhythm.
unfortunately, the sensation
gripping me most right now,
menstrual cramps, feels like
something completely alien
to my identity, *hostile*, crush-
ing my womb like a toothpaste
tube squeezing out its contents
in gobs. I concede the need to
affirm what is natural and by
tomorrow may,
but for
now
I'd
prefer
to
concentrate on
higher rhythms.

Earthmother

mountain of perfection
lady of bounteous beauty
with foothills of flowers   tranquillity of grasses
nestling men and wilder life in her fertile lap's fullness
arching over little ones   nursed at her springs
hums through scented tresses of wind-stroked trees
repose for the weary   mistress and challenge to the restless
lovers-plundered   roads laid through her
frost and thaw's sudden   erosions   the lost   burrowed into
her   bedrock   reliability   all   liberties
taken   with her   plenitude   she accepts
surmounts   seems to   grow   with time
multilayered   gives   and gives   herself
pleasing   all   who   use her   yet
heavy   with gut-held   mountain-needs
dumb reachings   burn   beneath surface   placidity
years adding to   adding to   add   until
molten heart   trembling   shuddering   suppressed
irrepressibly   tautens   convulsively   *erupts*
millennially-mute mouth   gapes   open
screams out in fiery speech.

femininity

the female body is slender, flesh
tenderly yielding, diminutive features
glow for others' pleasure, naturally
draw attention like all lovely
delicacy. soft-giving form
with unbolted portal, opening exposes
woman's innermost chambers,
for tenderness aching,
hardens against force.
her hair a loose-waving pennant
alluring capture by grasping hands.
femininity supplies no fortifications
its treasures decay in life's long
siege, crushed to rubble under the male
fist—becomes hate.

close

they bound as one into the subway
far beyond their years foul-mouthed
fan through, spread their legs
occupy the escalating car.
        jerked curve
and a woman wrenched from her support
flies in an arc past the sole tentative hand
crashes onto seated strangers. a roar
of beasts sighting a stricken goat;
suggestively blood-red her face, and dangerous tears
she barely escapes at the next stop,
as they surge into the aisle, flinging themselves
into mocking falls, screeching malevolent glee
while domesticated others unfocus their eyes
to withdrawn feet, camouflaged
they hope
until the pack moves on.

to iago internalised

twenty-one years you have accompanied me
present at my risings
precipitating my fallings
watching with the critic's supercilious smile
for mediocrity's inevitable pratfall
solicitously suggesting safer routes
than crossing rubicons.
your whispers confiding failure
on the stage even of my marriage-bed
more intimate than lover
penetrating the very marrow
of my incapacity.
insidious authority making
you the asp I suckle
as the forces unresistingly sink.
I have divided out my birthright
abdicated
hidden from the elements
denied myself thrice daily
betrayed my potential without a trial
unwittingly
murdered all but sleep.
now, tottering at the brink of tragedy
pillow already poised like a sword
I see you in me unmasked.
et tu Brute?
my kingdom for an ass?
am I to be or not to be?
out damned spot!

I have achieved the age of discernment.
it is time to consolidate my kingdom.

sisterhood

elusive words, my tools,
do not always serve,
too often their surface dulled
or imbalanced with clumsy connotations.
for those owed less
I have been able to chisel and polish
adequate gifts—
for you, never dared recompense,
my resources too raw
for the miracle of you.
memories I could heap up:
uncommon tears and laughter
of the nine years' rollercoaster ride
of our joint Lagos life,
shared fantasies, punctured pretences,
truth-telling of rare quality,
my body and spirit fed by every means
promoting health and growth.
no gift of equal value
to the unmeasured giving of your priceless self.
like tacky bric-a-brac proffered
in whimsical token of anything's
insufficiency, my words:
I love you
and thanks.

dismissed

want to run away home to mother
dead these twelve years.
how could she keep gone when I hunger so;
who will spread table before my enemies
again my wine has spilled away?

I sacrificed mother
to win back father.
he approved my lavishing help with her dying.
nursemaid to death I grew womanly;
faith was reborn
family embraced me
no more prodigal, I poured out my fullness
burying bad childhood in mother's grave.
but after she was disposed of
on the third day
zombie-raising father
exhumed it.
mother hadn't a word to say.

animus

my father's withering spirit possesses me.
denying his power
helped fulfil his damning prophecies.
opposition entrapped me deeper.
he incarnated in my husband
I fought again, and again fled.
animosity seemed to rule the world.
until at long last
tenderly touched by his antithesis
a miracle it seemed,
sterility gave birth to love.

then the quicksand of negation reasserted.
my gentle one donned the godmask,
casting out, deafly blaming,
merging with my accusers who are legion.
father of darkness eternally manifesting,
a blight to blighten the gentles.
once again I spread his spores of infection
even as I cry out to be saved.
exorcism!
open portals for entry of mother-spirit.

Type Cast

Archetyping

baby in glasses

you are very wise
not to rely on parents' eyes
it is they you need
most scrutinise.

Type Cast

Labels

When first I started working,
there were two toilets:
the Men's
and the Head of Department's.
We got that sorted out.

When first I entered the Staff Club,
everyone greeted me...
They said *Where's your husband?*
Now we women go in groups.

When first I gave birth to my son,
visitors called me *Our Wife*.
That meant they could tell me how many
more sons to have.

When first I went to the market,
sellers bawled out *Oyinbo*!
They still do. Growing old here
won't turn me black.

When first I gave students lifts,
they broke the handles off my car.
Now as I drive by they shout
Apartheid! CIA!

When first people told my daughter she was Igbo,
her retort *I'm an American!* galled.
Lately she's found a different response:
I'm not Igbo or American—
I'm me.

Archetyping

the Nigerian male

—interesting species this,
driven by an unusual instinct
for preservation of the female
whose independence he pities
and whose triumph over circumstances
reveals to him her need
for himself.

dehumanised

The worm inching its way in the dusky path
fails to look up or about,
dragging himself through the frayed bush,
scourged by the litter of refuse and stone
body desiccated,
spirit dead.

Yet, should he rear up
pierce the sullen miasma
and scatter the dust,
he would see his tracks infinitesimal
and the scrawny bush dwarfed
by overhanging and variegated palms.

But the worm never halts his self-appointed crawl
endlessly, obstinately self-expanding, self-
contracting,
eyes lowered, filming to opaque.
how terrible, that proudly impotent worm,
content to eat dust and bathe in the arid earth,
while around him the sky, filled
with the murmur of wings and song.

Archetyping

Quixote

Quixote thrusts his lance-lean form
through the random clutter of life.
he does not twice test his defences
(the helmet too laboriously made)
but unstintingly dares his very self,
his life assuming the shape of romance
even if others cannot see.
for them, work and prudence,
paying life's dues with common sense;
little men convinced there are no giants
and never were.
Quixote's enemies are real—
selfishness, oppression, cynicism, brutality—
and rule the world
which mainly in sleep still dreams of a champion
and healing balm.
the Enchanter, light-bearer,
exerts his dread powers
to rend power and glory
into confetti,
to darken to mere appearance a world
radiant with meaning and choice.
is vision
the passive reception of exterior impressions,
or the power to focus them
into purposeful harmony?
do we see with the vision
of Aristotle
or Plato?

the eye
or the entire, mysterious self?
was there truly in Aldonza
no latent loveable Dulcinea
undevised by the questing knight?
when he saw her steadily did he see her whole?
prudence cages Quixote and carts him home,
entirely animal.
repeatedly his friends defeat him
until bereft of vision
sane he lays himself down
in the security of bed
and life fails.
form and will collapse into chaos;
cackles echo in the darkness.

lessons

a neighbour-child calls beggars
Papa's friends
he never said to
love the poor
just gives in such a way
the child doesn't see
duty, deformity, grasping claws
he sees
friendship.

a mother teaches her child
charity and brotherhood
admirable ideals
the housegirl is very stupid
requires shouts to urge her on
today the child asks
seeking clarity
Children who refuse to go to school—
do they turn into housegirls?

time warp I

I was sitting in my bedroom
reading books from the '60's
and thinking about the revolution
that never came.

Thought about how if a Black Militant
were here right now
(if any of them are left)
he'd feel obliged to say *mothafucka* and scare me
and our worlds would never merge.
Me here
cut off
in my safe suburban nest.
Sighed for my milk-white
homogenised fate
looked out my narrow window
and saw
Africa!

time warp II

books stacked on every side
Black poets from the '60's
and the intricate pattern of hate
poems that kill
and deathpoems born in Malcolm's blood.
pawns aligned in military rows
from opposite chessboard positions.
every
thing
in black and white
I hadn't like the game.

my brown son of a black father
lifted one volume, asked
Who is this?
A black poet, I began,
wondering how to explain.
I didn't ASK
whether he was black or white...
—parents deal in evasions
and irrelevancies—
I asked WHO *he is.*

looking into my son's new eyes

under-cover

I brought in a morning glory
with visions of flowering vines
entwining with my courtyard pole.
Planted it, watered it,
and every morning for a week
the purple blossoms spread their glow
from the garden into my heart.
But their openness was but policy,
hiding the absence of root, and sapless stem.
One day they remained folded,
exposing the desiccation undisguised.
The flowers' arid beauty
mocked my response.

Perhaps I loved the morning glory
too quickly,
knowing her, like me,
to have prior existence in a faraway land,
luxuriant growth on gates
into childhood gardens of grace.
I, transplanted, sought likewise to grow,
to wrap a glory round my home.
rooting in the tropical soil,
drawing strength from the universal sun.
I did not want to believe
that one I care for
was so entirely
other.

to be come a man

exhaust-exuding time-battered taxi
bumper sign grates
to be come a man
is not a day job
each lone syllable a truth torn from life
by seared flesh,
recoil mastered by will.
starts up with the muezzin
yellow metallic shell of self
thrusts into hurtling currents
swooping, snatching, darting off
with morsels of sustenance
sun scorching, dust choking,
tumult seeping into the very blood
straining forward defies
the clogging flow,
necessity-driven
and laughter fuelled
with courtesy's saving remnant,
sun darkening, fuel burnt,
homing instinct at last let loose
serves wife and own wanting
another heat-stoking
thrust for perpetuity.
night's urge to balance rest and thought
sees unflinching through the dark
sameness stretching into fog of years
repetition without repose
sees, sleeps, rises

to repeat those night-known motions
drives / drives / drives
—a man.

the astute pickle

from his airtight bottle of vinegar
long since has disproved
logically–positively
the existence of sweetness and light,
permits himself the tiniest
soupçon of dill,
knowing in his sour preservative
nothing really is at risk.

prima donna

you the heroine of your own drama
ought to recognise there are other theatres
and performances than your own.
I have a lead part in a different story
though showing off-Broadway,
experimental, apparently formless, equally
eschewing glamour and formulas tried-and-true.
confounding public opinion's established taste
requires *sangfroid* daring, worth more
than glitter of your self-shaped acclaim.
experience playing one role
does not qualify you as insightful
on the painstaking rehearsals of another.

get off my stage.

glamour girl

the unformatted text of her shallow self
interested no one.
after consulting help
she learned to personalise her default setup
with selections from the style gallery,
embellished the body with clip art,
applied modish fonts
and boldfaced phrases.
she returned to the marketplace elaborately arrayed.
no takers.
despite chic layout, her text hadn't changed.

garbage in, garbage out.

Inside the Ivory Tower

deconstruction

categorical stands
soon require retrieval
of what remained seated.

D*E*E*P G*R*A*M*M*A*R

as we others (call us the
Ordinary Language Users)
thoughtlessly talked and wrote,
the methodical Linguist
fell into poetry in spite of himself,
discovering
        D*E*E*P G*R*A*M*M*A*R.

a convert from that moment
of revelational bliss,
renouncing the forms of
the old dispensation,
mysticism froze into dogma
as the Linguist created
Metalanguage, to commune
with the initiated few.

then inspired by missionary zeal,
the Linguist went out to preach his
omnipotent *Agent* and *Object*
        D*E*E*P G*R*A*M*M*A*R.
to all the nations
        to Anthropology
        Psychology
        Mythology
        Philosophy
        and Logic.
all saw the light and were born anew.

only the backward Isle of Literature

unscientifically clung
to its impressionistic rituals,
to doctrines primitive and old.
until one day thundering came
(in register for them appropriately low)
The Final Judgement:
People of Literature, I am sorry to say,
      you are...
      wordy.

the *Predicate* was immediately *Nominalised* into
      consternation
            supplication
                  and capitulation.
as there were no *Misinvocations*,
Misexecutions or *Abuses*,
the Linguist's *Performative Utterance*
was acceptance as *Felicitous* by all.

now most of the Isle sit *Patient* at his feet,
learning *Phrase Structure Commandments*
and intoning the Linguistic Creed:
            though we cannot yet see
            D*E*E*P G*R*A*M*M*A*R
            face to face,
            we believe in
            D*E*E*P G*R*A*M*M*A*R
            for we have seen His mighty
            Generative and *Transformational* works.

(abhorring wordiness, they omit the *Phatic*
Amen.)

Inside the Ivory Tower

On Teaching Afro-American Poetry to African Students

Me—
White lecturer
presenting and interpreting
the
Black
American
Experience
through lurid literary maps.
ANGER
laid open like jagged terrain
long departed
only half-known.
Impassive
Black faces
listening...
taking notes.

return of the lecturer

writers ambush
the American giant—
feverish rampaging Gulliver
trussed up by Lilliputians
wielding lances and scalpels—
sick giant
spewing bad blood.

I the hired guide
introduce touring students
to a few oblivious figures of note.
with my practised
academic
objectivity.

Before you,
guffawing, distraught,
is Twain
exposing and re-closing
boils under a loose flap of skin.
loosening the giant's strangling tie
and pulling off his trousers
where Hemingway
discovers the festering wound.
To his right, elbow-deep in pus and blood
is Faulkner, groping for something
obscured from student view
by his opaque form.
Steinbeck is the one weighing options

of milk and gun.
Over here, Ellison
rubbing paint-remover into
white-cataracted eyes.
Note the gentlemanly figure standing aloof—
James—polishing his poignard.
Slamming fists on the chest is Wright
trying to jolt
the stalled heart.
Busy at the mouth, Albee's
knife pins down the obstructive tongue,
freeing an agonised scream.

Delirious, the giant thrashes blindly
crushing one small tormentor,
Plath—Jong flies to fill the gap.
A few figures
sickened or exhausted
drift away
aiming infrequent arrows
or like Lot
not looking back.

Students gag at the stench
of bared rot
and let blood,
concluding
the Lilliputians hate
and rightly want to kill.

You misunderstand.
These violent assaults

are a form of love.
The hackers are
physicians
intense in their therapeutic incisions,
desperate as the disease.
For he is their
father—
I too his child.
Healed
the giant will live.

Home is where the doors close

The man who first asserted
home is where the heart is
was brother to the one who said
an Englishman's home is his castle.
Castles have moats around them,
drawbridges, garrisons,
and massive iron gates.
After strenuous years at the Crusades
he retreated to his heart's ease
(no matter whether castle or cottage)
and shut the door
with a thud.

Some centuries later
we pledged ourselves vassals of the
Might University Powers
who provided this lodging as fief.
In bygone days its numerous doors
stood stalwartly erect,
gripping their keys in pairs—
symbols of unfaltering vigilance
and conjugality.
At the height of our home's glory
lecturers-errant and their train
congregated here for refuge
and camaraderie.
When night came we bolted the entrance,
twisted the keys,
tested the doorknobs

then retired to our seemingly
inviolable bed.

But arch-enemy Time
who reduces even castles to rubble
has ravaged and crushed our defences.
The fierce cold jaws of a
harmattan morning
have cracked apart
the front door at its seams.
Two layers flair out now
from the exposed hollow core,
pennants of vulnerability.

Wayfarer, in quest of adventure,
halt briefly, explore this strange sight.
The gap under the door gave entry
to troops of pillaging termites,
who found hallway closet doors
perfect for a bivouac.
By the time their invasion was repelled
the foe had digested these doors
and conducted a foray
to the slats by the steps.

But bypass the termite catacombs,
the kitchen controlled by the audacious roach,
the disintegrating window screens
where claw-bearing felines
steal in through the holes,
and venture at once up the stairs
to see what damage Time has wrought

to the inner sanctuary.

The children's bedroom portal
from outside is deceptively inviting,
but abandon all hope
ye who enter here,
for the children's door closes
irrevocably.
There is no inside handle,
and at intervals children's
shrieks can be heard,
and agonised pleas for release.

Should you evade the maw of that
infernal gate,
and the pestilential miasma
from the bathroom domain
(where mute bewitched taps
and unflushable toilet
warn off all but the rash)
the most infamous door then accosts you.

The door to the master bedroom
turned traitor and defied us one day.
In order to win back his stronghold
the lord of the manor seized a machete
(no sword being in reach)
and broke its rebellion with a blow.
From then an implacable adversary
the door sullenly filled its function
and bided its time,
until one fateful evening,

vengefully disjointing its handles and latch,
the door made hostage of its liege.
The lord mustered his strength through the night;
his squire armed him
with a screwdriver at dawn.

Now all limbs amputated,
the door hangs a lifeless facade.
A hole the shape of eyeglasses
draws the intruder's prurient gaze.
Mosquitoes not only want to watch,
but also participate.
And any internal pant or sigh
sends the door drifting ajar.
Under such conditions, the lady of the house
(rather than the door) is
impregnable.

Wayfarer, wending your way,
carry news to the Powers
of their vassals' distress:
without demarcation
between private and public
the inhabitants' hearts
are demoralised,
for home is where the doors close,
and nature is more appreciated
outside.

The Wasted Year

1984

'Nígbàtí mo lọ sí Arò, mo rii pé wọ́n de olùkọ́ naà ní ṣékéṣéké lọ́wọ́ àti lẹ̀ṣẹ̀ wọ́n sì tì í mọ́ yàrá kékeré kan. Mo wá bèrè lọ́wọ́ olùkọ́ náà nkan tí ó fé. Ó dá mi lóhùn pé òun kò fẹ́ nkạnkan jù pé kí wọ́n fi òun sílẹ̀ síbẹ̀.'

For my colleagues

They endured.

I. *The Burial of the Failed*

June is the cruellest month, breeding
Exams out of the dead term, mixing
Memory and pretence, stirring
Dull minds with essays.
The session kept us safe, covering
Ignorance in packed halls, feeding
A little knowledge with dry lectures.
Finals surprised us, coming through the academic year
With the return of rain, we stopped going to classes,
And went out of campus, into the buka
And drank palmwine and talked for some hours.
Amaghi m ihe o bula gbasara Agumagu Bekee;
A bu m onye Naijiria.
And I was frightened. Staying at the hostel
We read, much of the night, and go to the library in the day.

What are the thoughts that clutch, what wisdom grows
Out of this baffling rubbish? English student,
You cannot say, or guess, for you know only
A heap of broken images, where metre beats,
And the dead notes give no help, criticism no relief,
And the dry text no sound of meaning. Only
There is shadow of understanding
(Come put in writing the shadow of understanding)
And I will show you something different from either
Your failure in Prelim striding behind you
Or your failure in final year rising to meet you;
I will show you fear in the coming results.

Sin me ke ukpeme fo
Kuyak odudu efen
Obo me ku ubok fo.

'You gave me invitations first a year ago;
'They called me the acada girl.'
—Yet, when we came back, late, from the Phoenician night-club,
Your pockets full, and your Peugeot wet, I could not
Resist, and my virtue failed, I was neither
Studying nor home, and I learned nothing,
Looking into the heart of romance, the presents.
me I no be gentleman at all o.

Nna Okechukwu, famous dibia,
Poor as he is, wisest man in Imo,
With his leather bag of *afa*. Here, said he,
Are your seeds, the sinking Igbo student.
Here is Isi Npume, the Goddess of the Stream,
Lady of artificial respiration.
Here is your man with three wives, and here his wheels,
And here is the four-eyed teacher, and these seeds,
A red mark, on a sheet she carries in her bag,
Which I am forbidden to see. I do not find
The First Class. Fear death by biro.
I see rows of numbers, circling round in a ring.
Thank you. If you bring me an all-white goat
Your enemies' witchcraft will be futile.
One must be so careful these days.

Unreal Lagos,
Under the brown dust of a harmattan dawn,
I had not thought F's had undone so many.
Each unemployed fixed his eyes before his feet.

There I saw one I knew, and stopped him crying 'Tunde!
'You who were with me in the Arts Faculty!
'That certificate you forged last year in your home,
'Has it given results? Will you work this year?
'Or has the sudden coup disturbed you too?
'O keep WAI far hence, if free you'd remain,
'Or your bad results they'll dig up again!
'You! hypocrite lecturer!—my grader,—my friend!"

II. *A Game of Charades*

The Chair she sat in, like a burnished throne,
Scraped in the office; on the blackboard,
Held up above a nonfunctioning phone
Reflecting candlelight upon the desk,
The glitter of her calculations rising
In rows of ivory and coloured chalk.
From the wastebasket poured in rich profusion
Unclaimed, her students' strange synthetic research,
Uncurbed, clumsy, or bogus—troubled, confused
And spurned all sense in hokum; swelled by hot air
So rudely forced; yet there the lecturer
Filled all the office with her despairing voice
And still she cried, and still she wrote down scores,
'F F' to bloodshot eyes.
Under the candle, she read exams, her hair
Stood out in fevered shock,
Reread their words, then would be savagely still.

'My scripts are bad to-night, Yes, bad. Stay with me.
'Reassure me. Why do you never reassure. Reassure.
'What are you thinking of? What thinking? What?
'I never know what you are thinking. Think.'
"We haven't had to think all this time
And it's too close to the end to start now."
'Do
'You know nothing? Do you see nothing? Do you remember
'Nothing?'
I remember
"*Tell Freedom* is authorbiography."

'Are you alive or not? Is there nothing in your head?'
                                                                                But
Uh-h-h-h... "Achebe's central theme is the Crash of culture."
    "Hester Prynne was impregnated and gave birth" I said—
I didn't mince my words, I said it to her myself,
HURRY UP PLEASE IT'S TIME TO COMPILE MARKS
"To a three-month baby girl."
HURRY UP PLEASE IT'S TIME TO COMPILE MARKS
"Jane Austen was a socialist writer."
HURRY UP PLEASE IT'S TIME TO COMPILE MARKS
HURRY UP PLEASE IT'S TIME TO COMPILE MARKS
Good night, exams, good night, sweet students, good night, good
    night.

III. *What the Exams Said*

After the horror red on sweaty faces
After the frosty silence in exam halls
After the agony in blue book answers,
The moaning and the grumbling
Protests and padding and dissimulation
Of English students over unlearned lessons
He who was learning is now dead
We who were teaching are now dying
With a little patience.

Here is no content but only sound
Sound and no content and the smeared ink
The words winding around about the answers
Which are answers of sound without content
If there were only content amongst the sound
Here one can neither read nor help nor pass
There is not even silence in the answers
But dry sterile chatter without sense
If there were content

And no form
If there were form
And also content
And content
A theme
Meaning among these sounds
If there were the sound of content only
But there is no content

In this decayed hole amid the Arts Block
In the full moonlight, the owl is singing
Over the tumbled scripts, about the office
There is the empty office, only the wind's home.
It has no lecturer; her mind swings,
Breakdown can harm no one.
Like a cock on the windowsill
She crows Eureka! Eureka!
In a flash of light—the exam answers
Making sense

The woman crouched, humped in silence.
Then spoke the exams
FLASH
Nye: what have we given?
Students, awe shaking my heart
The awful daring of Gatsby's rise to riches from rags
Which an age of snobbery can never retract
Except for the unfortunate fact of his death
When "he went from grass to grace and
Back to grass again." (Or alternatively,
"From grass to grease.") "He tried so hard
To get rich by hook or sink"—he died in a pool.
Melville's "Billy Bird", another giver with awful daring
Had a "kinsly relationship with Captain Vere,"
"Whose significance is outrageous."
"He was like Jesus who healed the woman
Torching his garments," though
It is not to be found in his obituaries.
FLASH
Nwee Obi ebere: I have found the key.

Too long has Claggart been blamed for
His treatment of Billy; the unfortunate
Man suffered from "natural deprivity."
Claggart heard the key
Turn in the door not even once only
Furthermore "Melville was biased against him."
Only just now these ethereal exams
Revive in Claggart a broken Coriolanus.
But Emerson even more, despite his
"Style of poetic illusion,"
Showed an exemplary sympathy when he taught
That "for a man to realise himself
He must sometimes leave
His own labour, to embrace
Other labourers"—which not
Even Whitman said at his most
Camaraderie*est*.
FLASH
Duzie: The mind responded
Gaily, to the hand expert with interpretation.
Jane Austen was a socialist writer, for
"Mr. Woodhouse threw dinners to his guests
And adviced them against their health."
His anti-bourgeois activity was underground;
No one suspected him till now.
"Mate-making" was Emma's anarchist contribution,
And "trying to sophisticate Harriet."
Emerson also represents elements of Control. His concept of
the Oversoul enabled him, within Unity,
To discover "multi-publicity," making him the world's first
Mass media and P. R. expert.
Had you heard his pitch

Your heart would have responded to the other labourer
Gaily, when invited, beating obedient
To his controlling hands.

I sat upon the floor

Doodling, with the padded walls around me
Shall I at least set my marks in order?
Nigeria airways puts you First, puts you First, puts you First
Ki ni ó ṣe pé o; ṣakará olojé ni.
Non cogito ergo non sum—O Mgbagbu ijiji
Dan Sofo ga mus ga mus Akata mato gan-ga-ga
These fragments I have shored against my release
Wetin woman fit do. Teacher don craze again o.
Nye. Nwee obi ebere. Duzie.

Ekim ekim ekim

NOTES ON *THE WASTED YEAR*

Not only the title, but the plan and a good deal of the incidental symbolism were suggested by Mr. T. S. Eliot's poem *The Waste Land.* Indeed, so deeply am I indebted, Mr. Eliot's poem will elucidate the difficulties much better than my notes can do; and I recommend it (apart from the great interest of the poem itself) to any who think such elucidation of my poem worth the trouble. To another work I am indebted in general; I mean the 1984 end of session examinations of our University of Lagos students; I have used especially quotations from students taking my "Introduction to the Novel" and "Nineteenth Century U.S. Literature" courses. Anyone who is acquainted with their work will immediately recognise in the poem certain modes of expression and thought.

Finally, I must express gratitude to my linguistic consultants, in particular, Prof. Abiodun Adetugbo, Prof. E.E. Okon, and the late Prof. Nnabuenyi Ugonna; the attitudes embodied in the poem are, however, not necessarily theirs.

Aro, mentioned in the Yoruba inscription, refers to the psychiatric hospital near Abeokuta, so renowned that in western Nigeria its name has become synonymous with mental illness.

Translation: "When I visited Aro, I saw the lecturer chained both by legs and arms in a small room. And I asked the lecturer what she wanted. She answered that she didn't want anything other than to be left where she was."

The quotation in the dedication to my colleagues is from William Faulkner's notes to *The Sound and the Fury*; see also his speech of acceptance upon receiving the Nobel prize for Literature in 1949.

I. THE BURIAL OF THE FAILED

Lines 12-13. Translating from the Igbo: "I know nothing about English literature; I am Nigerian."

28-30. Part of the first stanza from an Efik hymn:

Put me in your hands
Do not allow any other power

To take me from your hands.

38..Cf. Fela Anikulapo-Kuti's album, *Gentleman*.

II. A GAME OF CHARADES

Lines 87-8. My first year of teaching, when I told students that their examination would require not only memorisation but also thinking and applying concepts, one of them protested, "We haven't been expected to think all these years, and it's too close to exams to start thinking now."

93. This and all subsequent quotations and literary interpretations are taken verbatim from my students' June 1984 examination scripts.

III. WHAT THE SCRIPTS SAID

Line 146. *Nye*: Give (in Igbo).

162. *Nwee obi ebere*: Sympathise; literally, "have a heart of mercy."

181. *Duzie*: Control; lead in the proper direction.

202. Cf. Fela Anikulapo-Kuti's album, *Shakara;* translating from the Yoruba: "What did he call you; he's just bluffing"

203. The negative of René Descartes' "I think, therefore I am."

203. *Mbagbu ijiji* is Igbo slang for palmwine; literally, "the drowner of flies."

204. Fragment from a Hausa song: "The aged dances softly / Please hit the drum for her".

208. *Ekim*: Darkness (in Efik).